It is Saturday afternoon. Martin and his sister Pam are in Cambridge for the day.

They are looking at the beautiful old buildings of this University City.

Pam has a camera with her. She likes taking photos and sometimes they are very good and sometimes they are not very good

It is five o'clock. Pam and Martin are going home now.
They are tired after their long day. They are in the
garden near the bus station. "Let's have a last photo of
you," says Pam.

"Oh no, not again," says Martin.

"Come on," says Pam. "It's the last one. I want to finish
the film in my camera."

"Oh, all right," says Martin.

He stands in front of the flowers.

"Look at me," says Pam and takes a photo.

A man with a big rucksack on his back walks between Pam and Martin.

"Oh no," says Pam. "Now I've got a picture of that man, not of you, Martin."

The man looks at Pam. He is angry. He goes across the road without a word.

"That man isn't very nice, is he?" says Martin.

"No," says Pam. "And that was the last picture on the film, too."

The man with the rucksack on his back goes into the bus station. He has got sunglasses and a blue hat.

"Come on," says Martin. "Let's find our bus."

They go into the bus station.

"Look," says Martin. "There's that man again. He's getting into that bus. He's going to Aberdeen. That's in Scotland."

"Good," says Pam. "Far from here and far from me!"

She is angry with the man.

Three days later, on Tuesday, Pam has got her photos from the shop.

"Look at these," she says to Martin. "They're the photos of us in Cambridge."

"Oh, these are all very good," says Martin.

"But not this last one," says Pam. "Look, it's that man with the rucksack."

In the photo the man is in front of Martin. You cannot see Martin behind the man's rucksack.

"Wait a minute," says Martin. "I know that face. It's in the newspaper. Have you got it?"

"Today's newspaper?" says Pam. "Yes, it's here. Why?"

"Yes, here he is. Look at this picture," says Martin.

Pam looks at the photo in the newspaper.

"Who's that?" she asks.

"It says in the paper his name's Alan Rook," says Martin. "And he works in a bank in London. But on Monday morning – yesterday morning – no Alan Rook! The people at the bank don't know where he is. And they say he's got a hundred thousand pounds with him. The police are looking for him, too."

"But is that the man in my photo?" asks Pam. "He hasn't got a beard and he hasn't any hair."

"Look at his ears. Look at his nose," says Martin. "It's him. I know it is."

Martin has an idea. He takes a pencil and starts to draw on the newspaper.

"What are you doing?" asks Pam.

"Look," says Martin. "I'm putting dark glasses and a two-day beard on the man in this photo. Now I'm drawing a hat on his head. See? Now look at the two pictures."

"You're right," says Pam. "It's him. It's Alan Rook."

"Come on," says Martin. "Let's take these pictures to the police."

At the police station Pam and Martin speak to a policeman.

They put Pam's photo and the newspaper on the table and they tell their story.

"That's Alan Rook," says the policeman. "In Cambridge at 5 o'clock on Saturday. The big question is – where is he now?"

"We think we know. He's in Scotland, in Aberdeen,"
says Pam. "Or he's near there." They tell the policeman
about the man and the bus to Aberdeen.
"He's got a rucksack and a tent on his back in the
photo," says the policeman. "He isn't living in a hotel.
He's camping. If we're lucky, he's still in Scotland. I
must make a telephone call."

The policeman telephones the police station in
Aberdeen.

"Alan Rook's in Scotland," he says. "We think he's
camping near Aberdeen. He's got a short beard now."
The next day the police in Aberdeen find Alan Rook in a
tent in the mountains near Aberdeen. The money from
the bank is in his rucksack.

The next morning Pam and Martin's story is in all the newspapers.

There is Pam's photo of Alan Rook at the bus station.

There is a picture of Martin and Pam, too.

In the newspaper it says:

CAMERA GIRL GETS PHOTO OF ROOK

POLICE IN ABERDEEN FIND BANK MONEY

The people at the bank are very happy. They give Pam and Martin a thousand pounds.

"My last photo's a good one after all," laughs Pam.

"Now I can buy a very good new camera."

ACTIVITIES

Before you read

1 Look at the Word List at the back of the book. What are the words in your language?

2 Look at the picture on page 1. Answer the questions.

    a Martin and Pam are in Cambridge. Where is Cambridge?

    b Why is Cambridge famous?

While you read

3 Finish the sentences with one word.

    a Martin is Pam's ....

    b On .... , they take some photos in Cambridge.

    c At five o'clock they are near the bus ....

    d Pam finishes the .... in her camera.

    e A man with a .... walks in front of Martin.

    f The man gets on a bus to ....

    g Pam gets her photos from the shop on ....

    h Martin has a .... with a picture of a man in it.

After you read

4 Answer the questions.

    a What does Martin usually think of Pam's photos?

    b What does Pam think of the man with the rucksack?

5 Look at the newspaper on page 7.

    a What is the story in the newspaper?

    b What is Martin thinking?

Before you read

6 Answer the questions. What do you think?

    a Is the man in Pam's photo Alan Rook? Why?/Why not?

    b What can Pam and Martin do now?

While you read

7 Are the sentences right (✓) or wrong (✗)?

    a Alan Rook works in a bank.   .....

    b He has got some of the bank's money.   .....

    c The ears and nose are the same in the two pictures.   .....

    d Martin draws a beard on the man in Pam's photo.   .....

    e A policeman comes to Pam and Martin's house.   .....

    f Rook is sleeping in a tent in Scotland.   .....

    g The story of Pam's photo is in the newspapers.   .....

    h The bank gives Pam and Martin a new camera.   .....

After you read

8 Look at the fifteen pictures in the book again. Tell the story in fifteen sentences.

9 Write Alan Rook's story. Start: *Alan Rook works at a bank in London. He takes £100,000 from the bank. On Saturday, he puts the money in a rucksack and …*

10 Find a photo of a famous person in a newspaper. Write about that person. Put the photo on your paper.

    Start: *He/she is about ..... years old. He/she has .....*

WORD LIST *with example sentences*

beard (n) The man has red hair and a *beard*.

between (prep) B is *between* A and C.

camera (n) I want a photo of this place, but I haven't got my *camera*.

camp (v) They aren't staying in a hotel; they're *camping*.

city (n) London, New York and Tokyo are big *cities*.

draw (v) The little boy is *drawing* a picture.

ear (n) He can't hear with his left *ear*.

far (adj) Oxford is not *far* from London.

glasses (n) My eyes aren't good, but I can read with *glasses*.

last (adj) 31 December is the *last* day of the year.

mountain (n) Mount Everest is a very famous *mountain*.

nose (n) He has blue eyes, a long *nose* and a big mouth.

pencil (n) I haven't got a pen. Can I write with a *pencil*?

pound (n) Go to the bank and get fifty *pounds*.

rucksack (n) A *rucksack* is a bag for your back.

take a photo (v) Smile! I'm *taking a photo* of you.

tell (v) Can you *tell* me the name of this building?

tent (n) How many people can sleep in this *tent*?

thousand (number) 1,000

university (n) Oxford and Cambridge are famous *universities*.

Pearson Education Limited
Edinburgh Gate, Harlow,
Essex CM20 2JE, England
and Associated Companies throughout the world.

ISBN: 978-1-4058-6959-1

First published 1989
New edition first published 1998
This edition first published 2008

3 5 7 9 10 8 6 4 2

Copyright © Longman Group Ltd 1989
This edition copyright © Pearson Education Ltd 2008
Illustrations by Pat Foggarty

Typeset by Graphicraft Ltd, Hong Kong
Set in 12/20pt Life Roman
Printed in China
SWTC/02

Published by Pearson Education Ltd in association with
Penguin Books Ltd, both companies being subsidiaries of Pearson Plc

For a complete list of the titles available in the Penguin Readers series please write
to your local Pearson Longman office or to: Penguin Readers Marketing Department,
Pearson Education, Edinburgh Gate, Harlow, Essex CM20 2JE, England.